EXPLORING CAREERS IN TV AND FILM

Screenwriting

Jeanne Marie Ford

Cavendish Square

New York

Published in 2019 by Cavendish Square Publishing, LLC
243 5th Avenue, Suite 136, New York, NY 10016

Library of Congress Cataloging-in-Publication Data

Names: Ford, Jeanne Marie.
Title: Screenwriting / Jeanne Marie Ford.
Description: New York : Cavendish Square, 2019. | Series: Exploring careers in TV and film | Includes glossary and index.
Identifiers: ISBN 9781502641465 (pbk.) | ISBN 9781502641472 (library bound) | ISBN 9781502641489 (ebook)
Subjects: LCSH: Motion picture authorship--Juvenile literature. | Television authorship--Juvenile literature.
Classification: LCC PN1996.F64 2019 | DDC 808.2'3--dc23

Editorial Director: David McNamara
Editor: Kristen Susienka
Copy Editor: Rebecca Rohan
Associate Art Director: Alan Sliwinski
Designer: Christina Shults
Production Coordinator: Karol Szymczuk
Photo Research: J8 Media

The photographs in this book are used by permission and through the courtesy of: Cover, Mark Poprocki/Alamy Stock Photo; p. 4 Steve Debenport/E+/Getty Images; p. 9 Universal History Archive/UIG/Getty Images; p. 12 Zuma Press Inc/Alamy Stock Photo; p. 15 Jannis Tobias Werner/Shutterstock.com; p. 18 Logoboom/Shutterstock.com; p. 20 GaudiLab/Shutterstock.com; p. 22 Steve Cole Images/Istockphoto.com; p. 27 Hero Images/Getty Images; p. 30 Melanie Lemahieu/ Shutterstock.com; p. 33 Jacob Lund/Shutterstock.com; p. 35 Taniavolobueva/Shutterstock.com; p. 37 Hans Blossey/Image Broker/Alamy Stock Photo; p. 39 Ysanne Slide/Moviestore Collection Ltd/Alamy Stock Photo; p. 40 Anthony Neste/The LIFE Images Collection/Getty Images; p. 42 Pixsooz/Shutterstock.com; p. 44 Chris Cooper-Smith/Alamy Stock Photo; p. 46 DFree/Shutterstock.com; p. 48 Pictorial Press Ltd/Alamy Stock Photo; p. 51 Eldar Nurkovic/Shutterstock.com; p. 54 antb/Shutterstock.com; p. 60 Antonio Guillem/Shutterstock.com; p. 63 Tribune Content Agency LLC/Alamy Stock Photo; p. 65 TeodorLazarev/Shutterstock.com; p. 71 James Worrell/The Image Bank/Getty Images; p. 74 Andrew Milligan/PA Images/Getty Images; p. 80 Sylvain Lefevre/Getty Images; p. 83 El Nariz/Shutterstock.com; p. 85 Axel Schmidt/AFP/Getty Images.

Printed in the United States of America

CONTENTS

Moviegoers enjoy a film
that resulted from a script.

CHAPTER ONE

Screenwriting 101: What's Your Skill Set?

You sit on the edge of your seat, mindlessly devouring a tub of buttery popcorn. You're captivated by a heart-pounding action sequence unfolding on the big screen as a movie soundtrack swells in the background. Thousands of people across the country are sharing the same experience, all because once upon a time, a screenwriter typed two words on a blank page: "Fade In."

What Do Screenwriters Do?

"To make a great film, you need three things," said legendary director and screenwriter Alfred Hitchcock. "The script, the script, and the script." Moving performances and skillful directing, exquisite costumes and gorgeous cinematography, cannot elevate a mediocre script into a classic film.

Most people can name their favorite actors. They know the names of directors they admire: Steven Spielberg, Spike Lee, J.J. Abrams. Screenwriters, on the other hand, toil in relative obscurity. While nearly every moviegoer can quote memorable film dialogue, many would be hard-pressed to name a single screenwriter.

Screenwriter is the job title traditionally used for those who write for film, or "the big screen." Film writers work in a variety of genres—drama, action, comedy, romance, documentary, and science fiction, to name a few. They might write commercial movies, which are shot on large budgets for release in movie theaters nationwide. They might write art films, which can be shorter and are more likely screened at film festivals and competitions.

Television and video writers are called scriptwriters. They write for dramas and situation comedies (sitcoms), live-action children's programming, and animation. Talk shows, award shows, news programs, and sporting events employ scriptwriters. Game shows need writers to script questions and the hosts' patter. Even "reality" television uses writers. Outside of the major networks and cable channels, many scriptwriters work for local talk shows and newscasts.

The need for scripted material is not limited to film and television. New media such as web series have created many new jobs for scriptwriters. Video games have grown increasingly complex and often employ scripted scenarios and dialogue. Marketing and advertising firms use writers to craft scripts for presentations and commercials. Educational and industrial training videos used in schools and businesses have long provided a steady source of employment for scriptwriters.

Writing Skill Sets

Certain writing skills, such as narration and description, are rarely used in the process of scriptwriting. Others, such as strong dialogue and story sense, carry extra importance in a medium where the only readers are the actors and people producing the show or film.

Dialogue

No matter their genre or audience, one skill that all scriptwriters must develop is a good ear for dialogue. While strong dialogue should sound like real speech, there are key differences. Daily conversation is often littered with pauses and off-topic digressions. In scripts, dialogue must be crisp, clean, and purposeful. Books and short stories afford authors the luxury of extended description, but the scriptwriter can use only action and speech to convey information. Exposition and characters' inner thoughts must be revealed in a natural-sounding way through dialogue.

Aspiring screenwriters must learn to become skilled listeners. Producer Barri Evins writes in *Script* magazine, a leading source for film and TV news and advice, "Writers known for their dialogue actively listen. They pay attention to voices, they eavesdrop, they recall patterns, phrases, distinctions, inflections." She continues, "But great dialogue is not transcribing. It is learning about how people talk in the real world and then distilling it into something better that reflects real life rather than imitates it."

Another way to hone dialogue-writing skills is by reading widely from a variety of genres and authors. Read books, plays, and short stories. Pay attention to how each form uses conversation to propel the story forward.

Stage plays are the forerunners of movies and follow a similar written format. However, they are constrained by set changes and the limits of stage magic. They typically have far fewer scenes than screenplays and are driven primarily by dialogue. Derived from silent films, cinema has evolved into a visual medium with more focus on action. Television, on the other hand, had its roots in radio and tends, like plays, to be dialogue-centric. A lower budget and a faster-paced shooting schedule also limit the expansiveness of the visual effects usually seen on TV.

Story Structure

In 350 BCE, the philosopher Aristotle identified the three-act structure of the ancient Greek stage tragedy. Its main components are: the introduction; the middle, which includes the crisis or central conflict; and the resolution.

Nineteenth-century German novelist Gustav Freytag elaborated on Aristotle's basic story structure. He added the rising action, or complication, which typically occurs at the end of the first act; and the climax, or turning point, which ushers in the falling action and denouement, or resolution. His model is known as Freytag's Pyramid.

Plays, novels, and short stories tend to follow the same plot paradigm outlined by Aristotle and

Gustav Freytag developed a plot model known as Freytag's Pyramid.

Freytag. Screenwriting guru Syd Field analyzed dozens of classic film plots. His 1979 book *Screenplay: The Foundations of Screenwriting* lays out his version of Aristotle's three-act structure as it applies to movies. Field notes that in a typical screenplay, one page equals approximately one minute of screen time. He identifies approximately how many pages are typically devoted to each act, from the "inciting incident" through the plot points at the end of each act. He also demonstrates how these precepts are carried out in several well-known films.

Like Field, aspiring screenwriters must be analytical readers of novels, short stories, and plays. They should also seek out and read screenplays. Some are available as published books; many can be downloaded from the internet, often for free. It is important to look for full screenplays rather than dialogue transcripts in order to study the formatting, stage directions, and medium-specific terminology.

Aspiring screenwriters must also dedicate significant time to watching movies and TV shows. That's right, watching TV is a crucial part of preparation for the job. Scott Myers writes on his *Go Into the Story* blog, "To be a successful screenwriter, you have to immerse yourself in the world of cinema. Even if your interests are narrow—you write Action genre or Thrillers or Family or Whatever—it is important for you to have a comprehensive, wide exposure to a lot of movies." He suggests beginning with the Writers Guild of America's lists of the 101 greatest screenplays and best-written TV shows.

High-School Opportunities

According to author Malcolm Gladwell in *The Tipping Point*, approximately ten thousand hours of dedicated practice are required to achieve mastery of any skill. Writing is no exception. Just as all writers should be voracious readers, they need to put in the time to hone their craft. High school might be the best time to begin cultivating a daily writing habit. Literary analysis and creative writing assignments in language arts classes serve as opportunities for students to gain awareness of story structure and to experiment with dialogue. This is also the time to ensure a solid foundation in grammar. Even though screenplays aren't meant to be read by their audiences, sloppy presentation will be a turnoff to potential producers and a barrier to success.

Activities such as the yearbook, school literary magazine, newspaper, or TV news also allow students to gain experience writing for authentic audiences. A typical high school television production class includes instruction in screenwriting craft and conventions. Students in these classes often write short films, commercials, or documentaries. They will also learn the basics of television production: camera angles, scene transitions, postproduction, and editing. Hands-on production experience is invaluable for screenwriters to gain a holistic understanding of the filmmaking process. Acting courses can help aspiring scriptwriters learn what it's like to perform someone else's words. Psychology courses can also shed light on human motivation and behavior.

Students interested in screenwriting should take writing-intensive classes in high school.

Writers who want to pursue specialized areas of scriptwriting should consider taking other relevant elective classes. For example, future news writers will want to study journalism. Prospective video game scriptwriters should consider courses in computer programming and graphic design. Those interested in writing commercials should study marketing and advertising.

After High School

Unlike more traditional careers, such as medicine or teaching, there is no single path to becoming a successful screenwriter. A college degree is not required for the job, although it may be beneficial. Interested students have a variety of options they can pursue. Some may choose to learn on the job in entry-level production positions, either locally or in the major production hubs of Los Angeles and New York City. Others may take unrelated day jobs and carve out spare time for writing on evenings and weekends. Still others will go to college to continue their academic studies.

Regardless of the path they choose, most beginning screenwriters find it helpful to familiarize themselves with the concepts presented in the most widely read books in the field. In addition to Syd Field's seminal works, they should consider adding the following volumes to their bookshelves: *The Art of Dramatic Writing* by Lajos Egri; *Adventures in the Screen Trade* by William Goldman; *Making a Good Script Great* by Linda Seger; *Story* by Robert McKee; *Writing Screenplays That Sell* by Michael Hauge; and *The Writer's Journey: Mythic Structure for Writers* by Christopher Vogler. Also, *Now Write!: Screenwriting*, edited by Sherry Ellis, offers a compilation of helpful exercises from leading screenwriters.

Self-teaching can be supplemented as desired by professional instruction in the craft of screenwriting. Industry heavy-hitters such as McKee and Hauge regularly teach seminars in major cities as well as online. Sites such as mediabistro.com and Gotham Writers' Workshop have similar offerings with more budget-friendly pricing. These courses can be valuable; however, they do not typically offer the kind of detailed one-on-one feedback provided in a traditional classroom setting.

Another good training option for many prospective screenwriters is the local community college. Two-year colleges often offer courses, certificate programs, and asssociate of arts degrees in television, film, or digital production.

Film School

College students considering careers in screenwriting have seemingly endless options when it comes to choosing a major. Every writer needs a breadth of knowledge and life experience. English and literature can be useful majors for aspiring writers, but there are many other possibilities. For example, Michael Crichton, who created the franchise *Jurassic Park* and the long-running TV show *ER*, went to medical school before he turned to writing novels and screenplays. His scientific training inspired many of his ideas and gave him the background he needed to flesh them out with accuracy and professional insight. David E. Kelley was hired as a scriptwriter on *L.A. Law* because of his background as a lawyer. He went on to create several popular shows, including *Big Little Lies, The Practice, Ally McBeal,* and *Picket Fences.*

Many colleges offer film majors, and most of these include screenwriting classes. A few even have full-fledged screenwriting programs. They may offer bachelor's degrees, certificate programs, and/or

Some colleges, such as Harvard University, offer film courses, majors, or PhD programs.

master's degrees. Some of the top film schools for screenwriters include the University of California at Los Angeles (UCLA), the University of Southern California (USC), Boston's Emerson College, New York University (NYU), and the American Film Institute. These schools are highly selective, and the instruction they provide from working writers in the field is as valuable as the industry connections they can offer to graduates seeking jobs in the entertainment business.

While film school has many benefits, there are also drawbacks to majoring in film. Nonentry-level jobs in entertainment can be scarce, so it is important to weigh the pros and cons of earning an expensive degree that may not lend itself easily to employment in other fields.

TV writer/producer Shonda Rhimes notes in an Anatomy of a Script masterclass that film school was "a great training ground." But she adds, "You pay a lot of money ... to be able to say that you went to USC, and then to be able to say that you have the contacts afterwards ... The thing that I felt most strongly about when I was there is that, if you couldn't write when you got there, you were not going to be able to write when you got out."

A Question of Character

Academic training aside, one of the most important traits of a successful screenwriter is self-discipline. A first, second, or third screenplay is more likely to be a practice exercise than a saleable product. Until a viable script has been finished, polished over time, and ultimately sold to a studio, the screenwriter is not paid for his or her work. Indeed, most screenplays are never sold. Writers must do the work first and foremost because they love it.

The ability to work well in isolation is important, but screenwriters also need good people skills. They must sell their ideas in meetings and hone the delicate art of compromise as they see their scripts through the development and production process.

Finally, screenwriters must possess resilience. Rejection is commonplace, even for established writers. Perseverance is key. A successful screenwriting career requires talent and hard work, as well as a healthy dose of good luck.

Many aspiring screenwriters dream of careers in Hollywood.

CHAPTER TWO

Working with the Same Goal

Many think of screenwriting as a solitary pursuit. In reality, it is anything but. Wide-eyed writers dreaming of a Hollywood career should first understand how the business works and what they need to do to "break in." They should also be aware of the odds they're facing. According to the Writers Guild of America, the number of professional scribes who have sold projects to major Hollywood studios and production companies totals about ten thousand. Of those writers, approximately 50 percent earn scriptwriting income in a given year. About 150 major motion pictures are produced each year. Given these numbers, it's clear that only the most dedicated and talented writers will make it in Hollywood. You may well be one of them. If you're not, remember that there are many available scriptwriting jobs outside of the Hollywood system.

Breaking In

For a scriptwriter, a portfolio of highly polished scripts is the equivalent of a résumé. Therefore, the

A writer trying to "break in" to the industry should write every day.

first step for a budding screenwriter is to generate such a portfolio through months and often years of serious writing. Some writers discipline themselves to produce a certain number of pages per day. Others snatch writing time whenever they can, whether on an airplane, in a coffee shop, or even poolside.

For writers who dream of having their screenplays produced as major motion pictures for nationwide release, the hardest part of the process is typically not writing the script; it's finding an interested party to produce it. Even lower-budget "indie" (independent) films, which are generally made on much smaller budgets for limited release, require a substantial investment.

For legal reasons, most production companies will not consider submissions from the general public. Industry agents serve as gatekeepers for the producers and studios who buy scripts and hire talent. If a screenwriter is represented by an agent, producers can assume a certain level of professionalism. Reputable agents are highly selective when signing new clients, as they make money only after selling a given project. Any agent who charges money up front for services such as editing should be avoided.

Many agents are also reluctant to read submissions from unknown clients. They often rely on referrals and recommendations from people they trust. Most major literary agents are located in New York or Los Angeles. Because the major studios are also concentrated around Hollywood, many aspiring writers relocate to the Los Angeles area early in their careers. Working in the business in any capacity can help them form relationships with agents, industry executives, and other writers.

The Film Development Process

The process of taking an idea from script through to a finished film, known as development, can be long and arduous. A large percentage of current Hollywood film projects are remakes, sequels, or adaptations of books and other projects. Many ideas also originate from producers, who provide the financial backing for films. These producers typically hire established screenwriters to take their concepts and turn them into full-length screenplays. Original screenplays that are not written under contract, also known as speculative (spec) scripts, thus represent a limited share of the projects being made into films.

A script must stand out to be noticed among the large number of screenplays submitted to readers.

Ken Miyamoto writes in his *Screencraft* blog that only sixty-one spec scripts were sold to major studios in 2017. However, he argues that these numbers don't tell the whole story. A spec script can open doors for writers even if it is never sold or produced. It can lead to writing assignments in film or other media, new working relationships, and future production deals.

Acquisition

Script readers, also known as story analysts, are employed by agents and producers to select the most promising spec scripts from the volume of submissions they receive. Many script readers are aspiring screenwriters themselves and have received specialized training in evaluating material based on the specific types of projects their bosses are interested in producing.

A script must captivate a reader's attention immediately. "If I'm not caught in the first five pages, then it's time to go buy popcorn," former script reader Janaki Symon tells Syd Field in *Selling a Screenplay:*

The Screenwriter's Guide to Hollywood. A sloppy screenplay riddled with grammatical or formatting issues is also unlikely to make it past the first reader and into the hands of potential agents or producers.

The readers' feedback, called coverage, typically includes: the logline, or a one-sentence distillation of the central premise of the story; a brief summary of the plot; and the reader's comments or impressions. Finally, it includes an overall assessment: recommend, consider, or pass on the project.

Projects that are recommended for further consideration by a studio are generally read by multiple executives and producers. If there is consensus that the project is a good fit, the writer will be offered a contract. Sometimes the production company purchases a script outright. More likely, a beginning writer will be offered an option contract. When a script is optioned, the writer is paid a fee in exchange for the rights to the material for a specified period of time. Books may also be optioned as studios consider adapting them into films or television shows. These option rights ensure that no other **studio** can buy the script during the course of the option period. At this point, talent may become attached to the project. In other words, certain actors or directors might sign contracts to participate in the film if it is greenlit (given the OK) and proceeds to production.

Having a script optioned by a Hollywood studio is a dream come true for many writers. However, the vast majority of scripts that are optioned are never made into movies. If the option expires and the script is not produced, the writer is free to try to sell it to another studio. If all of the proverbial stars align and the option is exercised, the screenwriter is finally paid the full script fee in addition to the compensation already received for the option. The film then proceeds to production.

The screenwriter's role in a film is often over before production begins. Syd Field writes in *Selling a Screenplay* about the option process: "Once you sign those contracts you don't own the material anymore. They do. You're simply a writer for hire. They can do what they want with it." In movies, the director has the ultimate creative control over every aspect of a project, from music to costumes to postproduction film editing. Writers who dream of shepherding their scripts through the moviemaking process should consider becoming writer-directors.

Studios and directors may ask for significant rewrites on a screenplay during the preproduction process. These are sometimes completed by the original writer. Often, new writers are brought in to "punch up" the dialogue or perform more major edits to the story. Professional editors called script doctors are frequently hired to complete rewrites requested by a studio or director. A script coordinator is responsible for tracking the edits from various sources and preparing the finished screenplay for production.

During production, the script supervisor is in charge of maintaining the integrity of the script. Script supervisors ensure that actors say their lines as written. Because scenes are typically shot out of order, script supervisors have the important job of tracking script continuity from start to finish. Script coordinator Cole Fowler explains in *Script* magazine:

> *For example, if there are certain props with restricted quantities mentioned like a gun, I will count how many times the gun fires and do my research on the type of gun. This helps ensure whether it makes sense to see the gun reloaded on screen and whether props is providing magazines for the actor to reload the gun.*

Script supervisors are also responsible for the show's timeline. Fowler explains, "If there are mentions of injuries or time-specific things, I document the progression of how these would heal through the following scenes/episodes."

The script supervisor works closely with the editors in postproduction to ensure that the director's and writer's creative visions are fulfilled in the final product.

Television

Many scriptwriters work in both film and television. While the writing process is very similar, the production process differs in many ways. TV series writers are expected to produce and edit material quickly. They must also master the specialized skill of writing in the voices of existing characters on established series.

The four major networks (ABC, CBS, NBC, and Fox), cable channels, and subscription services such as Netflix, Hulu, and Amazon all produce original television programming. The number of scripted series in production today is larger than it has ever been. Primetime series are generally divided into two broad categories: dramas, which are shot with one camera and are sixty minutes long (including commercials); and situation comedies (sitcoms), which are thirty minutes long and are typically shot before a live studio audience with three cameras.

Every new television series begins when writers pitch ideas to network executives. According to writer Alex Harvey-Gurr in the article "What You Need to Know About Pilot Season," each network hears approximately five hundred pitches in an average year and goes on to order about seventy original pilot scripts for primetime programming. About twenty of those actually become produced pilot episodes. Perhaps five to ten ultimately receive full series orders in the spring. The period from January to May, when these pilot episodes are produced, is known as pilot season.

The traditional network TV season begins in September and ends in May. Most shows run for twenty-two episodes per season, though episode orders for cable and subscription services are typically smaller. If ratings for a new program are poor, it might be canceled after a handful of episodes. Each spring, the network announces which shows will be picked up for the following season.

After pilot season comes staffing season. Each new show has to hire a team of writers to create the season's episodes. Existing shows may also make changes to their writing staffs at this time. The most influential writer on a TV show is called the showrunner, also known as the executive producer. Hiring decisions ultimately fall to the showrunner, who has as much control over the series' creative vision as a director does over a film.

During staffing season, agents submit their clients' best work to showrunners in hopes that these writers will be hired as part of a writing team. This work might include original spec pilots, plays, novels, screenplays, or spec scripts for existing shows that are similar in tone to the one being staffed.

Writing for television is a collaborative process. Everyone must work together to create a great TV show.

TV shows occasionally use scripts from freelance writers during the course of the season. However, the serial nature of most programs today means that showrunners generally assign scripts to their contracted team of writers.

The title of staff writer belongs to those on the team with the least seniority. Story editors have relatively more experience. The most experienced writers often have producer titles. Whereas producers in film are generally the financial backers, most TV producers are writers.

Inside the Writers' Room

The writing team works together to develop the overall storyline arcs for the series season. They typically sit around a conference table in the writers' room and pitch story ideas, with the showrunner serving as the final arbiter of what will happen.

Each episode is assigned to an individual writer. The team works together to establish the main story points, called beats, of the episode, often on a whiteboard in the writers' room. They "break" the story into scenes, with the writers' assistant taking detailed notes on each day's discussion. The episode's writer then completes an outline and receives feedback from the network and senior writers. Next, the writer is sent home to work on the script while the rest of the team gets started on the subsequent episode. The showrunner will edit the completed script draft, which continues undergoing revisions throughout the shooting process. Unlike in film where the writer is rarely on the set, TV showrunners supervise the entire production and postproduction process.

In sitcoms, the table read is another important step of the writing process. Actors read a draft of the script in front of the creative team. Writers take note of lines that fall flat and then work together to polish the jokes and make the script funnier.

WRITERS' ASSISTANTS

Writers' assistants are often the unsung heroes of TV writers' rooms. They work long hours for relatively little pay. In addition to taking detailed meeting notes, they are often asked to perform storyline research and even pitch their own ideas. They proofread scripts and outlines and distribute all rewrites.

Cydney Kelley has worked in both film and television, serving as a writers' assistant on shows such as *The Game* and *Zoe Ever After* and as script coordinator on the *Black-ish* spin-off, *Grown-ish*. She likens her experience in the writers' room to a writing workshop where she's had the opportunity to learn from the best in the business. She notes that she finds the rewriting process especially instructive.

Kelley's experience ultimately served as a stepping stone to scriptwriting assignments. She says, "I wrote a couple episodes, which I got to shepherd through production. Those were definitely among the highlights for me. From the writing of the scripts, to the table reads, to the production meetings, to ACTION! … and then eventually seeing it on television with "Written By: Cydney Kelley" on screen … It was a long, hard road, but so worth it and so rewarding."

Turning a screenplay into a movie is the
ultimate goal of most screenwriters.

Doing the Job

Twenty years ago, most aspiring screenwriters were at the mercy of Hollywood's gatekeepers. The majority of screenplays were destined to go unread and unproduced. Even if writers were able to raise the funds to make one of their scripts into an independent film, distributing it and attracting viewers was a daunting task. Today's screenwriters are fortunate to have many more options to take a finished screenplay from the page to the screen.

Technological Advances

The advent of inexpensive, highly portable video cameras and editing software such as iMovie makes it possible for home moviemakers to produce quality films on a low budget. Apps such as Animation & Drawing and Green Screen by Do Ink have vastly expanded the types of effects that can be implemented by amateur moviemakers who may lack access to high-tech equipment.

Relatively inexpensive home equipment and platforms such as YouTube have made filmmaking more accessible to today's aspiring screenwriters.

The Internet

The internet also provides an avenue for films and videos to reach a wide audience. Anyone over age thirteen can start a YouTube channel (with parental permission, of course). Millions of YouTube subscribers tune in to watch young people play video games such as *Minecraft*, perform sports tricks, or share makeup tips. While the majority of such popular channels present unscripted fare, web series also garner a significant amount of traffic.

Rhett McLaughlin and Link Neal are YouTube celebrities. They met in first grade in North Carolina and became good friends. They wrote a screenplay together at age fourteen and began filming it but threw in the towel after a few scenes. They went on to study engineering in college, where they were roommates. Years later, they started a YouTube channel to showcase their hobby, which was comedy. Their talk show, *Good Mythical Morning*, eventually attracted more than twelve million subscribers. Now that they had an audience, Rhett and Link decided to read their childhood screenplay aloud over the course of six episodes. Fans happily did the work of turning it into a video for them. Rhett and Link eventually quit their engineering jobs to focus full-time on their growing media empire.

Another popular web series, *Studio C*, originated as a sketch comedy series at Brigham Young University in Provo, Utah. Sketch comedies are often not fully scripted. Actors may receive a scenario or an outline and then be asked to improvise. Many comics trained in this tradition are therefore adept at both writing and acting. They must hone the ability to think quickly and riff off of one another. Improv classes and stand-up comedy can be good venues for young people to hone their comedy-writing skills. Getting involved with live theater is a good option for any writer who wants to see his or her scenes performed without mounting a full-fledged film production.

Making a film or a web series requires not only a commitment to immerse oneself in the filmmaking process, but it can also mean a substantial financial investment. More ambitious productions can require fundraising campaigns such as Kickstarter in order to raise the necessary cash. Having connections in the entertainment industry or a college film department can be a huge help. Many series on the internet are thus written, produced, and/or directed by students. Some colleges, such as Tufts and USC, have websites devoted to showcasing content created by students, including short films, comedies, and docuseries.

Film Festivals

Local and national film festivals also present excellent opportunities for burgeoning screenwriters who turn their scripts into produced films. These venues offer a community for exchanging ideas and viewing new work. Students who enter their films also gain exposure to real audiences. Recognition from judges may generate further prospects for education, advancement, and networking.

In 2017, students from Canyon Crest Academy in California won a grant from IMAX to write and produce two eight-minute documentaries and then

Film festivals, such as the Venice Film Festival shown here, allow screenwriters to share their work with the public.

had the chance to screen them publicly. Their teacher, Mark Raines, told the *Coast News* that the process of writing a documentary was challenging at first for students. "You get so much information, and you have to form a story out of that," Raines said. "With a narrative you create the story and write and shoot what you've written and designed. Documentaries are almost backward."

Student Reed Martin appreciated the opportunity to interact with the audience after the public screening. "They asked us questions about the films," he recounted. "It was fun to show off our work." Martin felt that the process of making the movies was challenging. Because one of the documentaries was about bees, Martin contended with a number of stings when trying to shoot close-ups. He learned that moviemaking was not as glamorous as he might have expected but more rewarding than he imagined.

Competitions, Writer Development Programs, and Classes

What if you've written a screenplay but are overwhelmed by the idea of filming it on your own? You can't upload a script to YouTube or submit it to a film festival. However, you can enter it in a screenwriting competition. The website moviebytes.com provides up-to-date information about contests open to students. Some of the best-known screenplay competitions include Scriptapalooza, the UCLA Extension Screenwriting Competition, and the Academy Nicholls Screenwriting Fellowships.

Young screenwriters embarking on TV careers should also think about applying to competitive talent development programs run by studios such as Disney, ABC, and Warner Brothers. In addition, the Television Academy offers a highly regarded internship program for college students.

Summer filmmaking programs for high school students have also proliferated in recent years. Many colleges, such as New York University/Tisch School of the Arts, UCLA, and Loyola Marymount, offer summer screenwriting intensives for talented high

Warner Brothers is one of many studios to run a respected talent development program.

schoolers. More traditional camps, such as Interlochen Center for the Arts in Michigan, the New York Film Academy, and The School of Creative and Performing Arts in Cincinnati, Ohio, also offer screenwriting sessions for teens. Some offer weekend classes as well. While these programs can be expensive, many offer the opportunity for students to receive college credit for their coursework.

Writing conferences aimed at young authors are widely available and tend to be more affordable than screenwriting intensives. They may not focus specifically on screenwriting, but they generally offer a variety of sessions on topics useful to all writers such as dialogue, world-building, plot, and characterization.

Writing the Screenplay

Many screenwriters initially script short films rather than full-length screenplays. These contain the same major story elements but tend to be more manageable projects for beginning writers and are also easier to turn into finished films. A short film is generally less than forty minutes, often significantly so. Most shorts are produced for the film festival circuit.

Writers' own interests will help them determine their screenplay's genre as they consider the most important question: What do they want their film to be about? High-concept ideas are those that are extremely original and have clear marketing appeal. The execution of a high-concept script can sometimes be less important than the premise itself. *Wall-E* is an example of a high-concept film. It's novel because

The Disney movie *Wall-E* is considered a high-concept film because of its unique take on a love story.

it is a love story featuring robots and also because it contains very little dialogue. By contrast, character-driven pieces tend to be more artistic than commercial in tone.

Beginning writers may dream of telling complex, layered stories, but they are advised to cut their teeth on more straightforward projects. Screenwriter Barbara Nicolosi notes that a writer's "passion project" is often too technically difficult for an emerging writer to tackle. "You're not good enough yet to take on a project of that scope," she suggests. Stories with complex story structures or requiring extensive research should wait, she advises, until the writer has taken the time to learn the basics of the craft. She suggests that the third or fifth script might be a better time to explore more ambitious ideas.

Tony Soprano (*center*) of *The Sopranos* was an evil yet relatable character.

Writers' life experience as well as their reading and viewing history will help them develop multifaceted characters. It is important for the protagonist to be likeable, but every character, whether a hero or a villain, should have both flaws and redeeming features. For example, Tony Soprano of the HBO series *The Sopranos* is a mobster. In one episode, he may be a brutal murderer. In another, he is relatable as a man prone to depression who would do anything for his family.

It may be helpful for the screenwriter to create a full biography for all major characters that includes minutiae from favorite food and color to the character's deepest fear and biggest dream. While much of this information won't find its way into the script, the writer should know as much about the characters' internal lives as possible.

Character growth over the course of the film should be motivated by conflict that is organic to the story the writer wants to tell. While the conclusion should not necessarily wrap up the plot in a tidy bow, it should be satisfying for the audience.

Plotting

Sometimes a screenplay concept begins with a character; more often, the writer starts with the plot. Early in the process, the concept should be distilled into a logline. The brief show and movie descriptions in your TV's channel guide or on screen before you select a Netflix or Hulu program or movie are loglines. A sample logline from filmdaily.tv for *The Lion King* reads: "Lion cub and future king Simba searches for his identity. His eagerness to please others and penchant for testing his boundaries sometimes gets him into trouble."

Writer Graeme Shimmin posits a formula for creating an effective logline. He suggests identifying the setting (if it's noteworthy), protagonist, problem, antagonist, obstacle, and goal, and writing a sentence that brings this information together. Being able to identify these basic elements of the story from the beginning helps keep them in the forefront of the writer's mind at all times. The logline is analogous to the thesis statement of a research paper. Script analyst Staton Robin writes in *Script* magazine, "A one-, two-, or three-sentence story concept, properly

Revising and polishing your writing is a crucial part of the screenwriting process.

written, is the best tool you can possibly have to check out whether your story is working before you invest your time in writing a screenplay. Only when that concept is working perfectly as a 'map' for your plot ... should you go on to the next stage."

The logline serves several other purposes. It should be included in a query letter to an agent when a writer is seeking representation for a project. If given an opportunity to pitch an idea to an agent or producer, the writer should start with the logline.

As the plot begins to take shape, the writer quickly learns where more research is necessary. What kind of poison would the murderer use? What is the weather like in Alaska in July? Some stories will require much more time devoted to research than others. Writers must be conscientious about "getting it right." Even a science-fiction project must be grounded in a consistent and believable universe. Otherwise, the writer risks breaking the audience's trust.

During the drafting process, the writer will have to make a variety of important decisions. Should the story be told in a linear or chronological fashion? Or would a more nonlinear structure work better, as in *Groundhog Day, Dunkirk, The Last Five Years*, or *Pulp Fiction*? With novels, the writer's creativity is the only limitation. In screenplays (even those that will never be produced), writers need to think about what can feasibly be accomplished. A full-length feature screenplay is about 120 pages, or two hours, long. Budget must always be at the forefront of the screenwriter's mind. Cliff-diving, exploding vehicles, or location shoots in New Zealand are probably out of the question for most student films.

While writers are often tempted to just sit down and start writing the screenplay—and this method does work for some—it's generally advisable to have a plan of attack for structuring story ideas into individual scenes. Many writers begin with a scene-by-scene outline or a beat sheet, which is a bulleted list of the major story points. Outlines and beat sheets are generally required in the TV writing room. Writers may deviate from the plan as they flesh out the script, but the outline helps keep the story on track.

Sometimes writers are also asked by producers to provide treatments, which are highly detailed descriptions of a single episode or film. They are

Both writers and directors may use storyboards to plan their work.

written in narrative format and are usually at least fifteen pages long. While some writers prefer to begin with a treatment, these are usually completed on assignment at the request of producers.

Storyboarding is another organizational technique that has its origins in animation. It is a visual way of representing each scene with illustrated boxes. Both writers and directors may use storyboards in different ways to help them envision how the story will unfold.

Tools of the Trade

With a story structure in place, the writer can finally sit down to write the script itself. Script formatting and screenwriting terminology are important areas to master. Writers must become comfortable using a host of abbreviations: for example, VO for voiceover, MOS for "without sound," or CU for close-up. They must learn to write sluglines, or the text that identifies the setting and time of each scene.

Sitcoms follow a different format from TV dramas, which have a different format from films. Each TV show also has its own stylistic idiosyncrasies. Screenwriting software can help writers organize ideas on virtual note cards and type their screenplays in the appropriate format. Final Draft and Movie Magic Screenwriter are two of the most popular screenwriting programs in the industry. Celtx and Amazon Storywriter are free tools that include many of the same features. Word processing programs include templates that can also do the job with a little more effort on the writer's part.

Storytelling software such as Dramatica is available to help writers plot their screenplays based on specific story-structure paradigms. Some creative types disdain such "cookie-cutter" approaches to plotting, but others find these tools helpful.

Screenwriters must strike a delicate balance in terms of the amount of information they convey in the screenplay. They are not the sole creators of a film. Stage directions should be clear but spare so that the actors have room to make their own character choices. Directors, costume designers, music supervisors, and lighting and set designers are among those who will want to bring their own creative vision to bear on the project.

SHONDA RHIMES

Shonda Rhimes sold her first screenplay shortly after graduating from USC's master's degree program in screenwriting. Its option expired, and it was never made into a movie. She continued working odd jobs before she snagged her first screenplay assignment.

Rhimes then sold a pilot to ABC about female war correspondents. Again, it never got off the ground. However, it provided her with the opportunity to pitch a new series, which became *Grey's Anatomy*. She

Shonda Rhimes is one of the most accomplished television writers working today.

went on to create other hits such as *Scandal* and *How to Get Away with Murder.*

Asked to give a commencement speech at Dartmouth University in 2014, Rhimes had some wise advice for graduates: "You want to be a writer? A writer is someone who writes every day, so start writing. You don't have a job? Get one. Any job. Don't sit at home waiting for the magical opportunity." Rhimes revealed that she'd never dreamed of being a TV writer. She wanted to be an acclaimed novelist like Toni Morrison.

"At film school, I discovered an entirely new way of telling stories. A way that suited me. A way that brought me joy. A way that flipped this switch in my brain and changed the way I saw the world. Years later, I had dinner with Toni Morrison. All she wanted to talk about was *Grey's Anatomy.* That never would have happened if I hadn't stopped dreaming of becoming her and gotten busy becoming myself."

Rhimes did not spend her high school years preparing to be a screenwriter. What she did do was read and write and create constantly. Her combination of passion, work ethic, and talent led to success.

A script should leave room for actors and directors to bring their own creative vision to the project. Here, actors from *The Big Bang Theory* film an episode.

Local Opportunities

The most important step future scriptwriters can take is to hone their craft. After that, it is useful to learn as much as possible about the business of making films and TV shows. While it may be easier for Los Angeles and New York residents to make contact with industry professionals, there are many opportunities for students no matter where they live.

The most important film industry publications are known as the trades. These include the *Hollywood*

Reporter, Variety, and *Deadline Hollywood*. Keeping abreast of the trades helps writers learn who's who in Hollywood; what upcoming TV shows and films are being produced by which companies; and what trends are emerging in the deals being made. Professional organizations such as the Writers Guild of America, the Academy of Motion Picture Arts and Sciences, and the National Academy of Television Arts and Sciences also have informative websites and many resources for those embarking on careers in film and television.

Perhaps most crucial for those living outside the traditional entertainment industry hubs is connecting with nearby television and film production outlets. Nearly every mid-sized city has a local news channel and/or a public television station. In addition to news, these channels may produce sports or talk shows and documentaries. In smaller markets, reporters and producers often serve as writers. However, larger TV stations employ dedicated news writers.

Working on high school TV programs is instructive, but even better is gaining experience with state-of-the-art equipment in a professional environment. Students should consider seeking entry-level jobs or internships to learn firsthand how real TV shows are produced.

School systems often have their own cable TV channels. MCPS-TV in Montgomery County, Maryland, is one that offers internships to high school and college students. They earn course credit as they learn on the job, performing tasks such as research, writing, hands-on production, and video editing. Former intern Barry Worthington says, "One of the best things about MCPS-TV is that they were not only supportive during my internships there, but they also gave me guidance afterward … and I still keep in touch with the staff to this day." Worthington has gone on to produce a TV news show, found a production company, organize film festivals, and work as an adjunct professor of film at local universities.

Students whose primary interest lies in film might also consider volunteering at film festivals or a local film office. These offices attract, coordinate, and promote productions filming on location nearby. While students aren't likely to get much, if any, writing experience from these types of jobs, they will gain an enhanced understanding of the business as a whole.

Local video production companies are another avenue to explore. Some specialize in unscripted content such as weddings, but there is a significant need in most communities for educational and industrial training videos, marketing materials, and local commercials. Many of these companies are relatively small and thus more likely to give students more significant responsibilities.

While most TV writers' rooms are located in Los Angeles, many primetime series and cable channels produce programming in other cities across the country. Students who live near a production location can add these employers to their list of potential job prospects. Large organizations such as museums, newspapers, and magazines may also offer internships in new media.

Finally, many cable stations provide public access television. Members of the public have the right,

Local television stations provide good job and internship opportunities for students who aspire to work in film and TV.

within certain guidelines, to produce TV shows using the station's equipment. The Alliance for Community Media provides a list of public access opportunities, information about getting involved, and even awards and scholarships for members. Subjects of some of the zanier public access programming have included dance parties, murderous puppets, and a multitasking man running on a treadmill while painting.

Local television is more than just a training ground for those interested in professional scriptwriting; it can provide a lifelong career opportunity. Jason Santelli, a professor of film and video production at Frederick Community College in Frederick, Maryland, estimates that approximately 50 percent of his students go on to work professionally in the field, most of them locally. He notes, "Film and video production is not limited to the 'Hollywood' industry. A lot of local businesses are in need of film and video professionals to produce content for their websites, blogs, and local television stations."

Video Games

For those who want to write video games, networking and hard work are also key. Writer Anne Toole says in the online article "How to Get Started as a Game Writer" that indie games can provide many opportunities. "You need to be willing to put in the time. Have a portfolio that shows you understand the medium. You don't write a novel and call it a game." She suggests creating mobile games with friends and seeking internships while still in school. Breaking in as a game designer might also be easier than starting as a writer.

Getting Started

Daily writing is a routine analogous to a workout. "Writing is both a pleasure and a struggle," says Akiva Goldsman, an Academy Award–winning screenwriter. "There are times when it's really aversive and unpleasant, and there are times when it's wonderful and fun and magical, but that's not the point. Writing is my job. I'm not a believer of waiting for the muse. You don't put yourself in the mood to go to your nine-to-five job, you just go. I start in the morning and write all day. Successful writers don't wait for the muse to fill themselves unless they're geniuses. I'm not a genius. I'm smart, I have some talent, and I have a lot of stubbornness. I persevere. I was by no means the best writer in my class in college. I'm just the one still writing."

Aspiring actors, lighting directors, or costume designers have to wait for a project to come along before they can practice their craft in a real-life setting. Writers are fortunate that they can create their own projects. They can write at any time and anywhere; those who are successful do exactly that.

All members of a production team must handle feedback and criticism at some point. Here, a manager and a presenter run through a script.

CHAPTER FOUR

Challenges and Setbacks

In the book *A Martian Wouldn't Say That!: Memos TV Execs Wish They Hadn't Written*, Leonard B. Stern and Diane L. Robison compiled an assortment of confounding script notes sent by TV executives to writers. The daily highs and lows of the business are perfectly encapsulated in this one: "We're canceling your program as of the 17th of next month. That allows you four more episodes. Keep up the good work."

Dealing with Uncertainty

Even the most successful screenwriter contends with variable income, difficult workplace politics, creative doldrums, and sometimes brutal criticism. A stellar career can end with no warning; a lackluster one can suddenly skyrocket. A writer may land a coveted staff job on a primetime show that's canceled after a single episode. The euphoria after a screenplay is sold can turn to dismay when none of the original dialogue makes it to the big screen.

Feedback

One of the most common mistakes eager young writers make is submitting material before it is truly ready for primetime. "Your first script is your worst script," writes Ken Miyamoto on his *Screencraft* blog. "You haven't had the time to hone your screenwriting skills, instincts, or style. You haven't had the time to learn the basic guidelines and expectations of the film industry. You haven't had the time to make those necessary mistakes and you haven't had the time to learn from them. The art and craft of screenwriting is something that needs to be cultivated."

Time spent networking and cultivating relationships usually results in one chance to impress an agent or producer. If that first impression isn't a good one, there may not be another opportunity. Never submit a subpar script to an agent or producer. Write, rewrite, and rewrite again.

A trusted writing group can help writers ensure that their script is in the best shape it can possibly be before submitting it professionally. One contributor to the *Screenplay Readers* blog writes that such groups can be valuable because "we watch films with *people*. When we talk about films, we talk with people. The isolated screenwriter banging away in a darkened room by herself … is in many ways a disconnect from the 'audience' or 'group participation' spirit which lies at the core of filmed entertainment." A group of supportive fellow writers can form a community that serves as a proxy audience. They offer suggestions on successive drafts until the screenplay is finally polished enough to be ready for the marketplace.

Writing groups are often formed through local colleges or literary organizations. They may meet in person or online. A group doesn't necessarily need to be composed of other screenwriters in order to be useful. Novelists, short-story writers, and poets can also offer insightful input. The key is finding a group that shares similar sensibilities and feels comfortable. Writers may have to try several before finding the right one.

Most high school writers have participated in peer review of essays in their language arts classes. Receiving criticism from classmates can be stressful. Sometimes their feedback is terrifically helpful. Sometimes it seems far off the mark. It can be difficult to know how or even whether to implement it. Ultimately, the writer has the final say in what feels right for his or her own work.

Not all writers find critique groups helpful, but it's important to get input from several trusted readers before submitting it professionally. Beginning writers often turn to friends or family members. Those further along in their careers may prefer to pay freelance story analysts or script doctors to provide coverage on a completed draft. They can then incorporate these suggestions into their revisions before submitting the script to a contest, agent, or producer.

Dealing with Rejection

After spending weeks, months, or years polishing a screenplay, every writer should be prepared for the high likelihood that it will be rejected. The vast majority of screenplays are never sold. Barri Evins writes in *Script* magazine, "They say love hurts, but rejection is soul crushing. Having your idea, your script, your passion project turned down is a unique kind of pain. It's personal. This is your baby. And someone just said, 'It's ugly.' Ouch."

The truth is, rejection is rarely personal. Moviemaking is, of course, a business. Often a project is rejected for reasons completely out of the screenwriter's control: the producer has recently bought a similar script or isn't taking on new projects in the genre or is leaving the business altogether.

As anyone who's ever been cut from a sports team or experienced a painful breakup knows, not taking rejection personally is much easier said than done. But successful writers use rejection to motivate themselves to work even harder. As Ken Miyamoto notes, if multiple producers have the same note on a script, perhaps they have a point. Maybe their feedback can be used to make a change that will result in a sale on the next submission. Maybe the script isn't being submitted to the right producers. Or maybe it's really not good enough or marketable enough or timely enough, but that doesn't mean the next one won't be. The only way to ensure a screenplay will never be produced is to stop writing.

The best cure for rejection is to keep submitting and, most importantly, keep writing. The sting does lessen a bit with time and experience. J.K. Rowling's first novel was rejected by publishers more than a dozen times. After the *Harry Potter* series went on to sell millions of copies and was adapted into multiple blockbuster films, Rowling wrote the first installment of an adult detective series. She submitted it under a pen name to see how it would be received by editors. Again, the rejections poured in. "A writing class may help," one said.

Rewrites and Notes

Most writers revise their screenplays dozens or even hundreds of times before submitting them. If an agent shows interest, more revision will probably be requested before the script is sent out to production companies. If the script is sold, still more edits will be required. Often, the final project will bear little resemblance to the writer's initial concept. While there are many types of writing where authors have nearly complete creative control of their final product, screenwriting is definitely not one of them. In film and television, compromise is the name of the game. A thick skin is a must.

An important part of the writer's job is to successfully implement revision requests during preproduction from producers, directors, and network or studio executives. Sometimes these notes may seem ridiculous, impossible to implement, or both, as in this network note excerpted in *A Martian Wouldn't Say That*: "Although Connie is a sociopath, make sure she's not without warmth."

Writers must ask tactful clarifying questions in order to figure out what a producer really wants, just as a student might have to do with a teacher's comments on the rough draft of an essay. They must be creative when it comes to implementing revisions that satisfy the note-giver without compromising too much of their original intent.

On rare occasions, writers are asked to make a change that they feel would completely undermine the artistic integrity of a piece. In this case, they must consider whether to pull out of the project. This is never a decision that should be made lightly. If such a situation arises, the writer should take time to cool down, seek other opinions, and consider all options. It's also important to know the legal ramifications of breaking a contract before quitting any job.

Fighting Stress

A TV show is a particularly fast-paced environment, and writers are frequently called upon to make changes on the spot: an actress is pregnant or has a broken femur or has just entered rehab. Perhaps the last episode went far over budget, so a car chase has to be replaced with a quiet scene of two people drinking

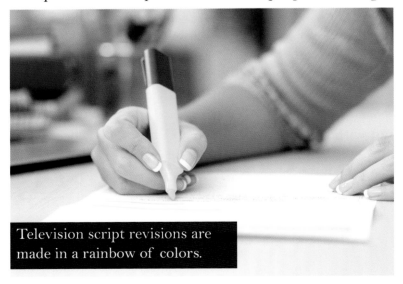

Television script revisions are made in a rainbow of colors.

tea. Perhaps the episode, which is supposed to run forty-two minutes without commercials, is fifteen minutes too long and needs major chunks of important dialogue excised. Perhaps an actor complains, "My character would never say that," and demands that his scenes be rewritten.

Script revisions are made in a different color for each draft, and the final shooting script is often more multicolored than a rainbow. The Writers Guild official list of draft colors includes such unique shades as goldenrod (for the sixth draft), buff (seventh draft), and salmon (eighth draft) The system used may vary slightly from show to show.

The fast pace of work in television, even on a high-school production, can be stressful. As most students know, learning to deal with pressure is key to success. Writer and therapist David Silverman explains in an article, "You have to come up with great ideas, and dialogue, and story ideas, and jokes on the spot. It's a lot of pressure, especially on your first staff job." He adds that some working environments are healthier than others. "Some showrunners will keep you in that room around the clock, all night long, until breakfast. Some will assign you to go off and write a scene, right now, and come back in an hour. Some showrunners will 'steal,' or 'co-opt' your story or writing credits, claiming they had significant input in forming your ideas. Sometimes they want their name on every episode in case it wins an Emmy."

In the writers' room, pitches are rejected regularly and publicly. When writers' ideas are shot down, they must quickly come up with new ones. If they are overruled about how a plotline unfolds, they must find a way to write the story with enthusiasm, even if it wasn't their favorite idea.

Silverman once worked on a series that satirized the rituals surrounding office work. "We would have story meetings on Friday nights," he says. "Once a story had been broken, the writer was sent off to write the sixty page script and turn it in over the weekend." He says that at that point, "Panic set in. After 48 hours of writing, judgment was passed on the script by the producers. If the producers hated it, you had to deal with the rejection and worry about your job, too. If you're lucky, and they liked it, you got a shot at doing the next rewrite. Add job insecurity and rejection to the list.

"I won't deny all these stressors had an impact on me. At various times, I was depressed, anxious, fearful, frustrated, and just about lost even caring about writing at all."

Silverman suggests setting small goals to make a looming deadline seem more manageable. His tips can easily apply to high school writers as well. Long stints writing alone should be balanced with time spent with fellow writers, friends, or family members. Take time out for meals rather than eating hunched over the computer and dropping crumbs on the keyboard. "Butt in chair" is standard advice for writers, who obviously cannot accomplish their work without spending large stretches of time at the computer. However, a sedentary lifestyle is a known health hazard. Don't skimp on exercise, which releases neurotransmitters that enhance mood. Many writers use treadmill desks or

Treadmill desks can help writers with sedentary jobs stay healthy.

bikes to ensure that they keep moving while working. At the very least, get up every hour and move around.

It's also important to establish good sleep habits. Poor sleep makes writers less productive. It will be even harder to meet deadlines if one falls ill, and sick days are not included in the typical TV writer's contract. Eat well and avoid caffeine. In short, practice good self-care, as everyone should make a habit of doing.

Carving Out Time to Write

Screenwriter Mark Sanderson writes on his *My Blank Page* blog, "The best discipline you can master early on is being mindful of time … As writers we must regard our writing time as precious and do everything in our power to protect our working time from the forces of interruption and procrastination. I know many non-writers who do not regard writing as real work and believe it's just playtime because it's creative." Anyone who has pulled out hair or shed tears over a high school research paper knows the fallacy of that argument.

"Consider writing a job," Sanderson advises. "This helps you to think of yourself as a professional." Professional writers who can't produce polished work in a short timeframe will lose their jobs. Developing the ability to work under deadline pressure is crucial. Procrastination is the enemy. Learn now to make writing time sacred. Avoid phones and social media, Candy Crush, and other distractions.

Sanderson points out that every writer is different:

The longer you write the more you'll get to know yourself better as a writer. You discover your strengths and weaknesses, if you write fast or slow, and if you're easily distracted or if you can work in a crowded coffee shop. When the writing gets difficult, time becomes your enemy as you never know each day if your creative juices will flow or dry up. Do yourself a favor and always protect your precious writing time from the forces of interruption. You'll keep on schedule, writing will become a habit, and you will be more productive than ever before.

Sanderson's guidance applies just as well to students, who already tend to be expert multitaskers and time managers. They must squeeze in homework after hours spent at school, sports practice, after-school jobs, babysitting gigs, and socializing with friends. Making still more time to read and watch films and write every day requires tremendous self-discipline. Those who are driven to make the time to do this are already on the path to success.

Writer's Block

Writer's block is the dreaded scourge of every professional writer. Students are familiar with the sensation as a paper due date looms: sweaty palms, stress, avoidance, and, in the worst-case scenario, a

It is important for working writers to develop strategies for dealing with writer's block.

missed deadline. In school, writer's block can result in a failing grade. For professional writers under contract, it can have much more serious consequences: a missed paycheck or a lost job. For those writing on spec, a promising project may be abandoned forever. When writer's block hits—and sooner or later, it does for nearly everyone—having a strategy to cope with it is key.

Stuart Perelmuter writes in *Script* magazine, "The degree to which a scribe can overcome block might be the difference between life as a career writer or a cater waiter. However, with advice ranging from 'just work harder' to 'take a nap,' and 'map it out' to 'preparation equals procrastination,' there is no one great cure-all."

Perelmuter surveyed a number of successful screenwriters about their approaches to either avoiding writer's block or addressing it if it does come to pass. Simon Kinberg says he spends 75 percent of his writing time on outlining and preparing. By the time he sits down to write the beginning of his script, "I have essentially already written the scene." Even then, he doesn't pressure himself to produce sparkling dialogue. The blank page can be daunting, and it's important to commit words to paper. He knows he will spend plenty of time revising and perfecting the draft later.

Perelmuter cautions, however, that "writers must be aware of the fine line between preparation and procrastination." Oscar-winning screenwriter Eric Roth says that research can sometimes be an avoidance tactic. He is wary of overplanning. He says, "I've written things where I've started off and gone halfway

DEALING WITH DISAPPOINTMENT: JOHN IRVING

John Irving is the author of acclaimed novels such as *A Prayer for Owen Meany* and *The World According to Garp*. He has achieved critical and commercial success as a writer through perseverance despite his severe dyslexia.

A huge film fan since childhood, Irving was thrilled when a studio asked him to adapt one of his early novels, *Setting Free the Bears*, into a movie. While he knew a great deal about writing novels, he realized he knew next to nothing about screenwriting. He was grateful to be paired with a partner, Irvin Kershner. According to Irving, "[Kershner] taught me how to write a screenplay ... He was my film school."

However, the project eventually fell through, as many film projects do. Irving lost the rights to the screenplay and was not even able to adapt his own novel for another studio. His hard work seemed to be for nothing. But rather than wasting time being discouraged, Irving called the experience "educative."

Years later, Irving was asked to adapt his book *The Cider House Rules* for the big screen. He was understandably reluctant to agree, but eventually he was persuaded. The laborious process took him thirteen years. The film went through four directors before it was made into a hit movie in 1999. Irving's patience paid off. The screenplay won an Academy Award in 2000.

through and said, 'This just isn't working.' Only then, with 60 pages or so written, can I start anew with a theme firmly grasped, ready to craft a story that is 'as good as you hope it can be.'"

Writers often divide themselves into two groups: plotters, or those who meticulously outline every part of the story; and "pantsers," or those who prefer to fly by the seat of their pants and make everything up as they go along. Ideally, most writers find a happy medium between these two approaches.

Having a disciplined writing habit can help keep the ideas flowing. When writers hit a wall, some find that it helps to get up, take a walk, and look at the script with fresh eyes after a short break. Some benefit from running ideas past friends and getting their input. Many find that a firm deadline is the ultimate motivator. The more a person is able to successfully work through writer's block, the less terrifying it becomes.

Rights and Permissions

Most students are familiar with the concept of plagiarism, or borrowing someone else's work or idea and passing it off as one's own. Even if accidental, plagiarism is an academic violation that can result in a failing grade or, at the college level, expulsion in the most serious cases.

In the professional world, stealing someone else's work, called intellectual property, has major repercussions. Most writers imitate aspects of projects they've admired, especially in their early writing. This act is called appropriation. Many writers will argue that there is no such thing as a truly original idea. Minor appropriation is not usually a problem. However, borrowing heavily from someone else's work without giving appropriate credit is the equivalent of stealing. Writers have been taken to court and ordered to pay large amounts in damages for projects that too closely mimic someone else's original ideas.

Some specific situations are considered fair use of copyrighted material. These include parodies. Parodies poke gentle fun at someone else's idea for comedic effect. The 1987 film *Spaceballs*, for example, parodied the well-known Star Wars films.

A writer interested in adapting a book or other work for the screen must obtain permission from that work's writer before undertaking the project. Generally, these adaptation rights are sold, sometimes for substantial sums of money. If a writer sells the adaptation rights to his own project, he is forbidden from adapting it himself unless he is able to regain the rights to it.

When turning a screenplay into a film, copyright issues can also be a concern from a production standpoint. The rights to music, for example, must be purchased, unless the material is no longer copyrighted and is considered to be in the public domain. Students working on school productions or films are expected to be aware of these legal copyright issues.

Equity

Like many other job sectors, the film and entertainment industry struggles to provide equitable job opportunities for all qualified employees. The majority of screenwriters are young, white, and male. This demographic also represents a disproportionate share of those in senior and hiring positions. According to the Writers Guild, in 2016, 29 percent of TV writers were female; 13 percent were minorities. The Writers Guild has consequently established special access projects for film and television writers in underrepresented groups: women, minorities, those with disabilities, LGBTQ writers, and those over age fifty-five. They offer staff writer boot camps and showrunner training programs to help writers and employers achieve more equitable representation behind the scenes. It is important for the creators of entertainment programs to reflect the diversity of experience of the audience and society at large.

Writers starting in the business are always well served to seek out mentors such as teachers and supportive colleagues. Shonda Rhimes credits producer Debra Martin Chase as an early mentor. Now Rhimes pays it forward by mentoring and nurturing those who work for her. In 2014, she received an announcement for an upcoming event she would participate in. According to an article in the *Hollywood Reporter*, "It called her 'the most powerful black female showrunner in Hollywood.' She crossed out 'female' and 'black' and sent it back."

Financial Planning

Showrunners like Rhimes are very well-compensated for their hard work. The Writers Guild minimum pay scale for a screenplay in 2017 was nearly $50,000. For a single sixty-minute TV script, it was $25,000. Most

Money management is a vital skill for people working in careers such as screenwriting that tend to have variable income.

writers negotiate significantly higher salaries than the WGA minimums. However, such seemingly generous compensation must carry writers through inevitable periods of unemployment.

Day Jobs

Very few beginning screenwriters are able to support themselves solely on the basis of their writing income. They need second and sometimes third jobs to keep themselves solvent, or financially stable. While these are commonly referred to as "day jobs," employment with flexible hours is the primary goal. Working three twelve-hour days or four ten-hour days allows more concentrated time for writing. Some aspiring screenwriters prefer to take mindless jobs to preserve their mental energy for their writing. Others seek industry jobs such as writers' or production assistant, agent's assistant, or script reader in order to make professional connections and learn on the job. The drawback to entry-level entertainment positions is that they typically pay poorly and involve long hours. On the other hand, they are often the best ways to open doors to promotions and permanent employment.

Working for a temporary agency that specializes in entertainment employment is often a good happy medium. These positions are short-term and allow greater flexibility than the grueling hours of most low-level Hollywood jobs. On the down side, they may not offer benefits such as health insurance.

During high school and college, it's a good idea to accumulate as many marketable skills as possible. If you have good administrative or computer coding abilities, if you can be a teacher or a massage therapist or a hairstylist, you will have more options when it comes to finding work to support yourself during lean times. No matter your aspirations, but especially if you're interested in a career in the arts, it's always helpful to have a plan B.

Money Management

Smart money management is important for everyone, but especially for people working in jobs with unpredictable income such as writing. After the euphoria of a first screenplay sale, writers may be tempted to quit their day jobs to write full time. They should resist, advises screenwriter John August on his blog. "There's no guarantee you'll have a second screenwriting job," he cautions. More practically, he notes that the first paycheck after a screenplay sale usually takes several months to arrive. When it does, a large chunk goes to taxes; 10 percent goes to the agent who made the sale; managers, lawyers, or accountants may take another bite out of the total; and dues will be owed to the film and TV writers' union, the WGA.

August advises writers to make one splurge after a major sale and save the rest of the money for a rainy day. Put six months' living expenses in the bank and invest the remainder. Don't touch it unless you really need it. Pay attention to the financial literacy training received in school, as it will come in handy.

Production assistants perform a variety of menial tasks, such as keeping actress Halle Berry warm on the set of the movie *Cloud Atlas* (pictured above).

CHAPTER FIVE

Applying Screenwriting Today

S creenwriting is a terrible way to make a living and I always try to talk anyone out of it," says screenwriter Amy Holden Jones, who was notably unable to take her own advice. Her writing career has spanned more than three decades and includes credits from the movies *Mystic Pizza* and *Beethoven* to the TV show *The Resident.* Fellow writer Robert Mark Kamen disagrees with Jones's assessment. "If you've got craft, you got game," he says. "If you got game, you can write your way in and out of anything. Writing is the best gig in the whole business, as far as I'm concerned. It's the only job where you don't have to wait for someone to tell you what to do." Regardless of whether aspiring screenwriters persist in the job, their training leaves them ready to take on the world.

Preparation Is Key

Production internships and entry-level positions involve a variety of menial tasks: making coffee, taking lunch orders, collating copies—the list goes on. An intern might even be asked to wash his boss's car or take the boss's dog to the vet. Even though these tasks may seem unworthy of a top graduate of a notable college, no one wants to be the assistant who crashed his boss's car or made her miss a flight to the meeting where she was about to seal a million-dollar deal. Yet such mistakes are inevitable, and assistants must learn how to handle them.

Anusha Deshpande, a writer and former production assistant, writes in *The Muse*, "As an assistant, you're in charge of so many logistical details that sometimes things fall through the cracks—and very often, things that are out of your control. The best thing to do is to figure out—and solve—those problems *before* your boss realizes your mistake. If it's too late and she's already discovered that you booked her car to the airport at 11 p.m. instead of 11 a.m. (true story), remember that she doesn't really care whose fault it is. It's your problem to solve. And it should have been fixed five minutes ago. So, assume things will go wrong. And when they inevitably do, stay calm and work hard to figure out a solution."

Deshpande notes the importance of asking for clarification when a direction might not seem to make sense. It's worth the risk of annoying a boss with a question to prevent a misunderstanding that might cost time and/or money down the line. Taking responsibility when mistakes happen and being ready, willing, and able to fix them is one of the most important traits of a good employee and citizen.

Flexibility and Creativity

Kristen Hewitt is a TV sports journalist. She thrives on the excitement of her job, but sometimes unanticipated excitement can be nerve-wracking. Early in her career, Hewitt was prepared to interview several basketball players for a news segment. She carefully researched the players' biographies and tailored her questions to their individual backgrounds. She anticipated what their answers would be and was already planning how the final product would look.

At the last minute, the media relations firm sent a different group of players for Hewitt to interview. Her script was suddenly not helpful or relevant. Hewitt panicked. Her segment was supposed to air the next day, and she had no idea what to do. She writes in the *Huffington Post*, "I had to fill a four-minute hole in the show. I looked at my veteran photographer with my eyes wide with terror and he said, 'No one at home knows what you planned. Change the segment, improvise. You just have to just roll with it.'

"I exhaled, nodded and did just that. I've never forgotten that day or the conversation Mike (my photographer) and I had afterwards in the edit suite. No matter what you've planned, life happens and things change. You have to change your expectations and work with it ... period."

Hewitt has carried this lesson into not only her work but also her home life as the mother of small children. When rain spoils an outdoor birthday party and a child is in tears, the ability to change the narrative is crucial. Television and film work teaches creativity, flexibility, and on-the-spot problem solving that can be applied to nearly any situation.

Teamwork

Working on a film or TV production is a powerful demonstration of the value of teamwork. In a pressure-filled environment, relationships can become strained. Personalities and styles clash. Learning to work through these differences is vital in nearly every job.

In the blog post "How to Work and Survive in the Film and TV Industry: The 10 Commandments of Filmmaking," veteran director and current film educator Peter D. Marshall writes, "I have learned many things during my career in the film industry, but one of the most valuable lessons I have learned was to remain human at all costs. And by this I mean to treat others as you would like to be treated yourself."

The majority of bosses got their starts in the business as lowly assistants. Some remember their humble beginnings and treat employees with compassion and respect. Others remember being taken advantage of and consider poor treatment a rite of passage. They behave as their bosses once did, making life miserable for their employees.

Working in the entertainment industry can be extremely stressful. While there are no life-or-death stakes attached to doing the job well, there is a great deal of money on the line. Furthermore, hundreds or maybe even thousands of people want the job you have and would be willing to do nearly anything to get it. While many circumstances will be beyond your control, you can vow to conduct yourself professionally and always treat others with respect.

Hollywood egos can be notoriously large. Writers compete fiercely for the same limited positions. Yet many find the generosity of spirit to mentor others. The ability to work well with others is noticed, appreciated, and ultimately rewarded.

Adjusting Expectations

Kristin Twiford had always wanted to be a reporter. She majored in media studies at the University of Virginia, where she worked for the campus radio station and completed a New York internship. Soon after graduating, she was offered her dream job as a reporter for a local TV station. After a year in the job, she came to a surprising realization: "I thought being a reporter was my calling. But when I finally got my shot, I realized reporting didn't make me happy."

Some stories were exhilarating. Many were tragic. Asking grieving families to speak to her was part of an important public service. It could also feel intrusive. It was difficult not to become too emotionally involved in her work. Twiford says that ultimately, "I realized I did not want to go on TV at the end of a every long and stressful day. You have to love being a reporter, because it's a really tough job. And I didn't love it enough.

"It's hard to accept that your dream job isn't your dream anymore. But you have to be true to yourself … I'm not saying I had the wrong dream. I wouldn't change a thing. My first dream job taught me lessons

I'll carry with me my whole life. I have new dreams now, but I will always be grateful for that first one."

Transferable Skills

Many screenwriters never achieve the Hollywood success they've dreamed of, but this hardly means they've failed. Through their training, they've amassed skills that are valuable in many other careers.

Communication

Effective written and oral communication are foundational skills in nearly every job. Sales and marketing jobs require employees to develop a strong

A camera crew films scenes from the 2017 movie *Dunkirk*.

GREA WARNER

Grea Warner knew she wanted to be a writer from the time she began scribbling in a diary. In high school, she took every communications and language arts class available. In college, she wrote and produced her own multi-episode series. She interned on a network television series and eventually moved back to her hometown to write and executive produce a local television show. She enjoyed her work, but as the years went by, she found that it sapped her creative energy. Finally, she decided it was time for a career change. Warner had always enjoyed working with kids, so she enrolled in graduate school to become a teacher.

Warner's professional background gave her a strong foundation for teaching writing. In the classroom, her enthusiasm was contagious as she worked to develop innovative projects and authentic writing experiences for students. Warner turned books into readers' theater scripts for them to perform. She taught them the joy of writing through journaling, letting them celebrate their creativity.

Working with kids was exhausting, but it fed Warner's soul. She maintained a strict writing routine in her spare time. Her television experience had taught her to be deadline-oriented and to value research and attention to detail. She continued to plot her novels as though they were scripts. "I write scene by scene in paragraph style," she says. "Then I write the dialogue in script style and, finally, I mesh it all together." Warner now is a published author. She continues to write daily.

rapport with potential clients. A nurse calming an upset patient and a teacher cajoling a kindergartner to do his homework know the importance of the art of persuasion. Word choice and creativity are key. Poor communication, on the other hand, is costly to businesses. It can result in job turnover, lost income, and even workplace injuries. Hiring managers value applicants who have strong communication skills.

Screenwriters are trained to excel at writing speeches in the form of dialogue. In the business world, the ability to script effective presentations is highly valued. Many fields, such as education and law, need workers with strong public speaking abilities. Likewise, clear and concise writing is important in nearly every career.

Screenwriters can easily transition into jobs such as script analysis, production, marketing, and teaching film at the high school or college level. Amy Gershwin is one example. She attended UCLA as an English major and obtained a master's degree in screenwriting from Columbia University Film School. At Columbia, Gershwin produced her own film projects, including an award-winning short.

Gershwin worked as a screenwriter for years. "My professional trajectory shifted," she explains, "when I was lucky enough to find an opportunity to produce commercials for an advertising agency. I did not know very much about advertising, but I did know how to produce short films, and luckily the skill set is basically the same."

She cites the ability to organize and multitask as key qualities in both jobs. Making her own film projects as a student gave her the technical skills she needed to be

Strong written communication skills are necessary in many jobs, especially in business professions.

an effective commercial producer. Her screenwriting experience also taught her how to be flexible and solve problems that might be encountered on a location shoot. She could do a quick rewrite on the spot to save the company time, money, or both. Like Gershwin, many screenwriters take on second careers that continue to make use of their scripting skills.

Discipline, Deadlines, and Perseverance

Karl Iglesias writes in his article "How to Become a Screenwriter: 6 Essential Habits of Highly Successful Screenwriters" that screenwriter Ron Bass "works an average of 14 hours a day, seven days a week." Eric Roth, meanwhile, "likes to wake up in the middle of the night, write for a few hours, take a nap, start again in the morning and continue in the evening."

Iglesias says, "Highly successful screenwriters are the most disciplined people I know. They make the time to write, face the blank page, produce a consistent amount of pages every day, and deliver high quality scripts on deadline."

Hard work, self-discipline, and the ability to reliably meet deadlines are qualities prized by employers everywhere. Job descriptions continually stress the importance of being a "self-starter." Intrinsic discipline is especially important for those interested in starting their own businesses.

Iglesias points out that screenwriters are trained to exercise discipline even when they don't get immediate results, in the face of rejection, disappointment, and long odds for success. He says, "Successful screenwriters adapt to the realities of the system and generally accept its flaws. They understand it's still a medium driven by stars and directors, that their work will get rewritten, that they'll get fired without knowing it, and so on. They know the only control they have is the quality and output of their pages."

Screenwriter Greta Gerwig tells the *New York Times*, "I have gotten into baseball recently, and whenever I have trouble writing, I think about the pace of baseball. It's slow. You strike out a lot, even if you're great. It's mostly individual, but when you have to work together, it must be perfect. My desktop picture is of the Red Sox during the World Series. They aren't winning; they're just grinding out another play. This, for me, is very helpful to have in my mind while writing."

Optimism vs. Realism

New York Times best-selling author Ally Carter notes on her blog that the majority of her successful

Screenwriters Manuel Alcala (*right*) and Alonso Ruizpalacios (*left*) hold the Silver Bear award for Best Screenplay at the Berlin International Film Festival in February 2018.

writer friends have projects that have been optioned in Hollywood. However, most will never actually become films.

"Basically, the odds of getting a movie made are long," she writes. "The odds of getting a GOOD movie made are miniscule. But we keep trying."

Writers must possess boundless optimism in order to pursue their dreams. It's important to keep driving toward an attainable goal. It's equally important to deploy clear-eyed realism, to know when to let go and set a new goal.

In his article "Lessons Learned from Winning a Screenwriting Competition," David Flores writes, "Years ago when I received word that my screenplay, *Control; Alt; Delete*, had won not one but two screenwriting competitions, I believed that all the hard work, years of struggle, self-doubt, and rejection had culminated to a glowing achievement that would forever wash away the specter of failure: I had climbed the mountain to see my shining new horizon as a working screenwriter. And it was marvelous."

His dreams had come true. His was a Hollywood success story. Then, gradually, his situation changed. He lost his agent and his manager. The screenwriting assignments stopped coming. Flores was devastated. Could he even call himself a writer if he was no longer making a living from his writing?

Flores ultimately realized that second-guessing the decisions he'd made was getting him nowhere. Part of success, he decided, was dealing effectively with failure. He began turning his scripts into comic books and publishing them. It wasn't the screenwriting job he had always wanted. It didn't pay as much money and wasn't quite as glamorous. But it was satisfying work. He continued to tell stories. He was able to call himself a working writer again.

"The point is," Flores says, "always move forward no matter what mistakes you make or rejections you encounter. This is your story—how you end it is up to you just as long as you keep writing it."

Like Flores, many aspiring screenwriters find that they need to reevaluate their dreams—often multiple times—over the course of their careers. Those who can be flexible, adapt, and keep working at their craft will find success, even if it doesn't happen quite the way they imagined it would.

GLOSSARY

adaptation A movie made from a book or other property.

appropriation Borrowing ideas from another person's work.

attached Contracted to appear in a project.

beat A story point.

continuity Consistency of props, wardrobe, story, etc., from scene to scene.

coverage A reader's description and evaluation of a screenplay.

denouement The resolution of the story.

development The process of acquiring a screenplay and turning it into a movie.

exposition Background information and explanation.

fair use Permissible use of another person's copyrighted material.

franchise A group of popular entertainment properties that may include sequels and merchandise.

freelance Work performed by someone who is not a permanent employee.

greenlit Approved to proceed to production.

high-concept Material with a highly original and marketable idea.

indie An independent film not made through a major motion picture studio.

logline A one-sentence summary of a TV or movie concept.

networking Getting to know other people in the business to advance one's opportunities for success.

option A type of contract that sells rights to a screenplay or idea for a certain period of time.

parody A work that makes gentle fun of another work that preceded it.

pilot The first episode of a prospective TV series.

pitch The process of presenting a story idea for consideration.

primetime Nighttime television, usually between the hours of 8:00 p.m. and 11:00 p.m.

public domain Material that is no longer protected by copyright.

right Legal permission to use certain material.

showrunner The head writer/executive producer of a television show.

slugline A line in the script that gives the location and time of a scene.

spec script A script that is written without an assignment or guarantee of compensation.

storyboard A visual representation of a film's story structure.

table read A stage in the sitcom writing process in which actors read an early draft of the script aloud.

treatment A detailed narrative summary of a screenplay.

FOR MORE INFORMATION

Books

Field, Syd. *Screenplay: The Foundations of Screenwriting.* New York: Delta Trade Paperbacks, 2005.

Hamlett, Christina. *Screenwriting for Teens: The 100 Principles of Scriptwriting Every Budding Writer Must Know.* Studio City, CA: Michael Wiese Productions, 2006.

Lanier, Troy, and Clay Nichols. *Filmmaking for Teens: Pulling Off Your Shorts.* Studio City, CA: Michael Wiese Productions, 2014.

Snyder, Blake. *Save the Cat!: The Last Book on Screenwriting That You'll Ever Need.* Studio City, CA: Michael Wiese Productions, 2005.

Trottier, David. *The Screenwriter's Bible: A Complete Guide to Writing, Formatting, and Selling Your Script.* Los Angeles, CA: Silman-James Press, 2014.

Websites

Drew's Script O-Rama
http://www.script-o-rama.com/snazzy/dircut.html
This website includes links to downloadable film and TV scripts that writers can study for format and content.

So What Exactly IS a Film Producer?
https://www.nyfa.edu/student-resources/so-what-exactly-is-a-film-producer
This article from the New York Film Academy describes a producer's role and contains links to other jobs in film.

Student Screenplay Contests
https://www.moviebytes.com/student-screenplay-contests.cfm
This website provides information about screenwriting contests for students.

Videos

How to Make a Good Script Great with Linda Seger
https://www.youtube.com/watch?v=-lpN5B-zS6E
This video shares tips from well-known screenwriting instructor Linda Seger.

PBS: Youth Filmmaking Programs
http://www.pbs.org/pov/filmmakers/resources/youth-filmmaking-programs.php
This website lists filmmaking programs that are available to students.

Writing a Bulletproof Screenplay That Sells
https://www.youtube.com/watch?v=xnaVYtCHs6U
This video shares tips from well-known screenwriting instructor Michael Hauge.

Online Articles

Buchman, Eric. "Anatomy of a TV Writers' Room." Bunch Notes. February 6, 2014. https://buchnotes. com/2014/02/06/anatomy-of-a-tv-writers-room.

Grove, Elliot. "10 Things Filmmakers Should Know About Screenwriting." Raindance. August 24, 2012. https://www.raindance.org/10-things-filmmakers-should-know-about-screenwriting.

McIntosh, Steven. "Toronto Film Festival: 7 Screenwriting Tips from Aaron Sorkin." BBC. September 9, 2017. http://www.bbc.com/news/entertainment-arts-41211061.

"101 Greatest Screenplays." Writers Guild of America West. Accessed March 28, 2018. http://www.wga. org/writers-room/101-best-lists/101-greatest-screenplays.

"6 Essential Screenwriting Tips for Writing Better Movie Dialogue." Stuidobinder.com. Accessed March 23, 2018. https://www.studiobinder.com/blog/6-essential-screenwriting-tips-for-writing-better-movie-dialogue.

INDEX

ABOUT THE AUTHOR

Jeanne Marie Ford is an Emmy-winning television scriptwriter and holds a master of fine arts degree in writing for children from Vermont College. She has written numerous books and articles on a variety of subjects. She also teaches college English. She lives in Maryland with her husband and two children.